Neuter

Is a

Gender

Identity

-By Laurel Federbush

Not "he" or "she," but "it." Some of us identify as being neuter.

Passive...

What does that mean? It means being an object. A useful object, ideally a prized and cherished one. A treasure.

Subservient...

Passive, receptive, docile, submissive. Not all the time, and not with everyone. Probably not with most people, since you can't survive in the world without standing up for yourself. But we feel aligned with who we truly are when we are willingly compliant.

Malleable...

We feel most alive when
being treated as an
inanimate object.

Subject...

We are there to serve others, passively, by being acted upon. Not to take center stage. Not to be the focus of anyone's affections.

Donation...

Independence is not the goal, although that's often where we find ourselves, since we don't fit into the current relationship paradigms.

Portable...

We don't seek to be equal.

We seek to be of service.

Useful...

We don't find ourselves represented in popular culture. Only occasionally does something even suggest our kind. We suspect we must be very rare, but it could be that we're good at hiding, meek as we are.

Soft...

We have so far been left out of gender identity politics. Which is okay with us, since we don't seek the spotlight.

Inert...

But we ought to make ourselves known, since we suspect that others would benefit if we were truly allowed to be ourselves.

Property...

This is not self-denigration.
This is who we are. We can't
be otherwise.

Tractable...

Being an object more than a person, or more accurately, being a person who is an object, is our natural state. Not a sex object, just an object.

Specimen...

Some examples, maybe...

Priced...

Used as a tool, a means to an end

Owned...

Acted upon as raw material,
or traded like goods

Item...

Bought and sold as
merchandise, or given as a
gift

Available...

Inert as a piece of furniture, content to be your footstool

Tagged...

Owned as property, even
passed along to the next
generation as inheritance

Fertile...

Boxed and shipped like a package

Possession...

Studied like a specimen, a research subject

Delivered...

Viewed as an exhibit, or
displayed as an ornament

Branded...

Not just instrumental, but actually an instrument

Salable...

A project to be worked on

Material...

A game to be played

Unobtrusive...

A good-luck charm, or a prize to be won

Receptive...

A canvas to paint on

Article...

Something for lovers to carve their initials into

Acquisition...

A meal to be feasted upon

Tool...

Spare parts, just in case

Shipped...

Whether or not the pronoun "it" ever replaces "he" or "she" in our vocabulary to refer to individuals like ourselves by our choice, it would be good if our existence were recognized, since we're here and want to be useful in whatever way we can be.

Chattel...

Esteeming ourselves is recognizing what (not who) we are. Reclaiming our inner "it."

Treasure...

You can have your pride parades. We'll be the floats for you to ride on.

Object...

We're "it." Being a thing can be a very cool thing to be!